OWYA

PRIMARY SOURCE DETECTIVES

WHO BROKE THE WARTIME CODES?

Nicola Barber

Heinemann
LIBRARY
Chicago, Illinois

To contact Capstone Global Library, please
call 800-747-4992, or visit our web site
www.capstonepub.com

Edited by Andrew Farrow, Patrick Catel, and
 Vaarunika Dharmapala
Designed by Steve Mead
Original illustrations © Capstone Global
 Library Ltd 2014
Illustrated by HL Studios
Picture research by Ruth Blair
Originated by Capstone Global Library Ltd
Printed in China

17 16 15 14 13
10 9 8 7 6 5 4 3 2 1

**Library of Congress Cataloging-in-
Publication Data**
Barber, Nicola.
  Who broke the wartime codes? / Nicola
Barber.
     pages cm.—(Primary source detectives)
  Includes bibliographical references and
index.
  ISBN 978-1-4329-9606-2 (hb)—ISBN 978-1-
4329-9613-0 (pb) 1. World War, 1939-1945—
Cryptography—Juvenile literature. 2. World
War, 1939-1945—Electronic intelligence—
United States—Juvenile literature. 3. World
War, 1939-1945—Electronic intelligence—
Great Britain—Juvenile literature. 4.
Cryptographers—United States—
History—20th century. 5. Cryptographers—
Great Britain—History—20th century. 6.
Cryptography—United States—History—
20th century—Juvenile literature. 7.
Cryptography—Great Britain—History—20th
century—Juvenile literature. I. Title.

  D810.C88B36 2014
  940.54′8641—dc23
2013015848

Acknowledgments
We would like to thank the following for
permission to reproduce photographs:
Alamy pp. 13 (© Tim E White), 44 (© Pictorial
Press Ltd), 51 (© AF archive); Corbis pp. 11
(© Bettmann), 20 (© Edifice), 35 (© Hulton-
Deutsch Collection), 37 & 42 (© Bettmann),
46 (© Alessia Pierdomenico/Reuters); CRIA
Images p. 30 (Jay Robert Nash Collection);
Getty Images pp. 19 & 36 (SSPL), 26 (The
National Archives/SSPL), 27 (Buyenlarge),
55 (Hulton Archive); Mary Evans p. 7 (Everett
Collection); National Security Agency pp. 14,
15, 25 & 52; Superstock pp. 16 (The Francis
Frith Collection), 57 (Science and Society);
The National Archives, ref. HW25/3 p. 23; The
National Archives, ref. HW 1/1 p. 41; Topfoto
pp. 5 & 22 (The Granger Collection), 41
(Topham Picturepoint), 49 (UPP); Wikipedia p.
28 (source unknown).

Cover photograph of the registration room
in Hut 6 at Bletchley Park reproduced with
permission of Getty Images (SSPL).

Page 56: Extract from *Colossus: The Secrets
of Bletchley Park's Codebreaking Computers*
by Copeland et al (2006). 133w from pp.
82–83. By permission of Oxford University
Press.

CONTENTS

Some words are shown in bold, **like this**. You can find out what they mean by looking in the glossary.

A DARING RAID

It is spring 1941, in the midst of World War II (1939–1945). At a secret location in the United Kingdom, thousands of men and women are working desperately to **intercept** and understand the **wireless** messages transmitted every day by the German armed forces. The Germans use a secret **code**—Enigma—to protect the information in their messages. Breaking this code allows the **Allies** to know what the Germans are planning—it is invaluable information. However, it is also very difficult to do.

RAIDS

The British code-breakers need to crack the German navy's codes, because the German **U-boats** (submarines) are a deadly threat to Allied merchant ships in the Atlantic Ocean. One of the code-breakers comes up with a plan to seize the settings sheets and one of the machines used to generate the code—an Enigma machine. These trophies would give them the clues they desperately need. In May 1941, in a highly secret operation, the Royal Navy manages to capture a German weather ship and seizes its settings sheets. They sink the weather ship, to avoid letting the Germans find out that the setting sheets have been taken. Then, only a few days later, British destroyers force a U-boat (U-110) to surface. Believing the U-boat to be sinking, the commander does not destroy his Enigma machine or its codes. They, too, are seized by the British.

HISTORY DETECTIVES: KEEPING SECRETS

The activities of the code-breakers remained secret far beyond the end of World War II. It was only in the 1970s that the true story began to emerge. Thousands of people kept their wartime jobs a complete secret from everyone, including friends and family. This book looks at how and when those secrets began to come out, and the story of what has happened since.

▲ This Enigma machine was used by the German military during World War II to encode wireless messages.

ULTRA SECRET

These are just two episodes in the secret world of code-breaking in World War II. Of course, all sides used codes, and all were trying to break each other's codes. This book, however, mainly examines the work of the Allied code-breakers in the two most significant operations. The first of these was Ultra, the name given to information obtained from the messages intercepted and **deciphered** by the British. The second was Magic, which was information gained by American code-breakers by intercepting and unscrambling Japanese signals. The huge value of both operations was that Germany, Italy, and Japan remained unaware that their codes were being broken. The name Ultra suggests this—it was considered even more secret than top secret! This was important and, as we will see, the Allies went to huge lengths to disguise and protect their code-breaking activities.

WHAT WERE WARTIME CODES?

Codes and **ciphers** have been used since ancient times. We know of secret codes used by the ancient Egyptians, Greeks, and Romans. The oldest known military cipher was the scytale, which dates back at least 2,500 years. Imagine a long piece of leather (or papyrus), which is wrapped around a piece of wood. A message is written on the leather along the length of the wood. Then the leather strip is unwound. It contains a meaningless jumble of letters—until it is wound around a piece of wood of exactly the same width, when the message is suddenly revealed.

The advantages of not giving away your plans to your enemy were also well understood by the ancient Roman military leader Julius Caesar. The Caesar cipher substituted letters by shifting the whole alphabet along, often by three places. So "a" became "d," "b" became "e," and so on. We know about this cipher and about the scytale from descriptions by ancient writers.

HISTORY DETECTIVES:
WHAT IS A PRIMARY SOURCE?

The Zimmermann telegram (see page 7) is an example of a primary source, a document that was written at the time being studied. It gives us firsthand information about an event or a period in time. Primary sources come in many different forms: "eyewitness" accounts, sketches or paintings, documents such as wills or telegrams, or, from more recent times, photographs or films.

You can find out more the Zimmermann telegram at www.ourdocuments.gov/doc.php?flash=true&doc=60.

THE ZIMMERMANN TELEGRAM

We are now going to jump to the early 20th century and a room in London, England, for the next example of wartime code-breaking. In this case, the interception and deciphering of a **telegram** changed the course of a war. Room 40 was the name given to the code-breaking section of the British Royal Navy, set up in October 1914, just after the outbreak of World War I (1914–1918). In January 1917, the code-breakers of Room 40 worked on the text of a telegram sent by the German foreign minister, Arthur Zimmermann, to the German **ambassador** in Mexico. At this point, the United States had not entered the war, although the Allies were becoming increasingly desperate for U.S. assistance. In his telegram, Zimmermann instructed the ambassador to suggest that Mexico join the war as a German ally. In return, Germany would ensure that the U.S. states of Arizona, New Mexico, and Texas would become Mexican territory.

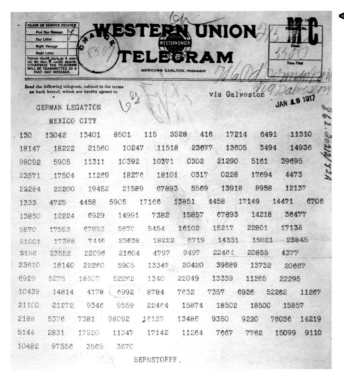

◀ This is the coded text of the "Zimmermann telegram," written by the German foreign minister Arthur Zimmermann to the German ambassador in Mexico, in 1917.

The full text of the telegram was published in the U.S. press on March 1, 1917. Zimmermann himself admitted that he had written it. The impact on American public opinion was immediate, and just over a month later, on April 6, 1917, the U.S. Congress declared war on Germany and its allies.

A NEW MACHINE

From World War I onward, a new technology—sending messages by radio—required new levels and techniques of secrecy. In 1918, a Swiss businessman, Arthur Scherbius, invented a machine to **encrypt** (turn into cipher) messages. He sold it to banks and businesses as a security tool and called the machine "Enigma." The German armed forces began to use a military version of Enigma in 1926. So, Enigma was not just one machine— it was a type of machine, and many Enigma machines were manufactured over the following decades.

SETTING THE SCENE

It is important to remember that all the events described in this book happened before the computer age, when the main forms of communication were radio and telephones with landlines, and all records had to be kept on paper.

HOW DID ENIGMA WORK?

The Germans believed their Enigma ciphers were uncrackable. They continued to believe this throughout World War II. The British and Americans were incredibly careful about how they used **intelligence** gained from deciphered Enigma codes, in order to keep the Germans using Enigma. What was it about this machine that gave the Germans such faith?

Scherbius's machine looked a bit like a typewriter with a keyboard. When the operator pressed a letter on the keyboard, the action moved rotors called "scramblers." Once a letter was coded, its cipher lit up on a "lampboard." The rotors moved every time a key was pressed, so the same letter would be enciphered differently. To decipher an Enigma message, the receiving operator needed to know the starting settings of the scramblers in the sending machine, as well as which rotors had been used, and in which order. With this information ("key"), and an Enigma machine, it was possible to unscramble the message. The Germans set daily "keys," which were distributed in codebooks. This is why the capture of codebooks (and Enigma machines) was so important to the Allied code-breaking effort.

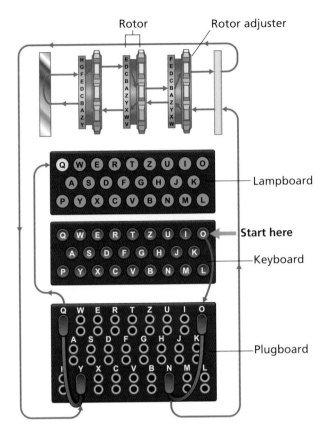

Rotor

Rotor adjuster

Lampboard

Start here

Keyboard

Plugboard

▲ This diagram of the Enigma machine shows the route of encryption from keyboard to plugboard, through the rotors, and back.

WHAT DID THE ALLIES USE?

Both British and American **cryptographers** developed their own **cipher machines**. The British adapted a commercial version of Enigma in 1934 to produce a machine known as Typex. The U.S. Army and Navy developed a machine in the 1930s called SIGABA. This machine was used successfully throughout World War II—as far as we know, its code was never cracked. During the war, it became necessary for the British and Americans to have a secure way to communicate top-secret information to each other. By adapting the SIGABA and Typex machines so they could "talk" to each other, a new machine was produced called the Combined Cipher Machine (CCM). The CCM was used from 1943 onward.

PADS AND POEMS

Not all wartime codes required the use of machines; for agents on the ground, it was necessary to have much simpler ways to communicate. The Special Operations Executive (SOE) was a secret organization set up by the British in 1940 for spying, **reconnaissance**, and **sabotage**. Its agents used various methods to disguise their communications, including the one-time pad and…poetry!

If used properly, the one-time pad is a cipher that cannot be broken. The "pad" usually refers to a small book of pages printed with sequences of random numbers. The code relies on both the sender and the receiver having the same pad and using the same page of numbers (the "key") to turn the message into code at one end, and to decipher it at the other. Once a page is used, it is destroyed. Because the key is random and used only once, it is impossible to crack this code.

However, it requires many pages of random numbers to make "keys," and it relies on both agents having and using the same key. Nevertheless, the one-time pad was used throughout the war, often with tiny letters printed onto pieces of silk that could be hidden in clothes and destroyed after use.

CODE-TALKERS

The need to make ciphers more secure against the enemy meant that even simple messages sometimes took hours to send. If speed was important, these time-consuming processes were not ideal.

In the United States, in 1942, an American civilian named Philip Johnston suggested a solution. He had grown up with the Navajo people in Arizona, and he believed their language would make an uncrackable code. It had no alphabet, and only people who had grown up with it could speak and understand it. In May 1942, a group of 29 Navajo recruits drew up a dictionary of code words. All Navajo code-talkers had to be able to recall every word of the dictionary instantly, even under extreme pressure. The system proved very valuable.

▲ Two Navajo "code-talkers" send a radio signal during the Battle of Bougainville in the Solomon Islands, in 1943. The Japanese were never able to break this code.

NAVAJO CODE WORDS

Many frequently used military words had their own Navajo equivalents. These are some examples:

America: ne-he-mah (mother)

fighter plane: dah-he-tih-hi (hummingbird)

submarine: besh-lo (iron fish)

tank: chay-da-gahi (tortoise)

WHO WANTED TO BREAK THEM?

In the years between the two world wars, code-breaking became very important, as suspicions about other countries' motives grew stronger. In 1926, the code-breakers in the British navy's Room 40 began to pick up German messages that they could not decode. Neither the Americans nor the French were able to crack the messages either. This was the beginning of the Enigma story.

POLISH CIPHER BUREAU

Polish code-breakers made the first breakthroughs. Poland, like France, was feeling increasingly threatened by Germany, particularly because of German ambitions to regain territory it had been forced to give up after World War I. The Poles set up a Cipher **Bureau** to monitor German communications. They, too, experienced the perplexing new code used by the Germans after 1926, but they persisted in their attempts to break it. The Polish code-breakers were helped by information about the Enigma settings that was sold by a German informer and passed on by the French.

Throughout the 1930s, the Polish code-breakers Marian Rejewski, Henryk Zygalski, and Jerzy Rozycki worked on the Enigma code, painstakingly analyzing data and building **replica** Enigma machines. They were successful, but they constantly had to find new ways to break the codes, since the Germans devised methods to make the machines more secure. Then, in 1939, extra levels of security introduced by the Germans finally put an end to the Polish success—they simply did not have the resources to tackle the problem.

A SURPRISE

At the same time, the situation in Poland was becoming critical, as it became clear that German invasion was imminent. The head of the Polish Cipher Bureau, Lieutenant Colonel Gwido Langer, invited representatives of the British and French intelligence services to a meeting in Poland. The British and French were astonished to learn that the Poles had been deciphering German messages for years; they had assumed that the Enigma cipher was uncrackable. The work of the Poles gave the Allied code-breakers an invaluable head start when war did break out, with the German invasion of Poland on September 1, 1939.

WHO IN HISTORY

MARIAN REJEWSKI
1905–1980
BORN: Bydgoszcz
(Bromberg), Poland

ROLE: A mathematician by training, Rejewski broke Enigma codes in the 1930s. In 1939, he escaped to Romania and then to Paris, where he worked once again on decoding Enigma messages. From 1940 to 1942, he was part of a secret intelligence unit in occupied France. He ended up in the United Kingdom in 1943, where he once again worked on decoding. After the war, he returned to Poland, and to the family he had left behind there.

Did You Know?

Rejewski's contribution to the Enigma story remained a total secret until the 1970s.

BLACK CHAMBER

A Cipher Bureau was set up in New York City in 1919. Known as the "Black Chamber," this highly secret organization broke the codes that were used by many countries, including Japan, to protect diplomatic communications. In 1928, Herbert Hoover became president of the United States, with Henry L. Stimson as his secretary of state. Despite its successes, Stimson decided to shut down the Cipher Bureau. His reasons included the need to save money and a desire to encourage trust between countries. He declared: "Gentlemen do not read other gentlemen's mail."

YARDLEY'S REVELATIONS

The head of the Cipher Bureau, Herbert Yardley, found himself unemployed and unable to find another job once the bureau was shut down. It was the start of the **Great Depression**, and Yardley soon found himself running out of money. So, he decided to tell all. In 1931, he published a book, *The American Black Chamber*, detailing the activities of the bureau—its successes, its techniques, and how it was organized. The book caused an uproar. Stimson denied ever having heard of a Cipher Bureau. The Japanese were outraged that

▲ Herbert Yardley was head of the Cipher Bureau until it was shut down in 1929.

their diplomatic codes had been broken. They immediately tightened up the security of all their codes, in addition to introducing cipher machines for the first time. In the United States, a direct result of the book was the passing of new legislation (An Act for the Protection of Government Records) in 1933 to make sure no one ever revealed this sort of information again.

Loyal or disloyal?

There have been many debates about Yardley's motives for writing his controversial book. Yardley had been working for an organization that did not officially exist, and he found himself without an employment history when the Cipher Bureau was shut down. Therefore, money was clearly a factor. But he also claimed that another motive had been to alert the United States to the importance of code-breaking and the weakness of its own systems—as he put it, "America's defenseless position in the field of **cryptography**." What do you think? You can find out more about Yardley at: www.nsa.gov/public_info/_files/cryptologic_spectrum/many_lives.pdf.

ARMY AND NAVY

At about the same time that the Cipher Bureau was closed down, the U.S. Army set up the Signal Intelligence Service (SIS). William F. Friedman was the leader of this new organization. Its purpose was not peacetime code-breaking, but rather training code-breakers in preparation for war and preparing codes for use by the U.S. Army. Meanwhile the U.S. Navy had its own code-breaking unit, called OP-20-G, which was mainly involved in intercepting and decoding the communications of the Japanese navy. The intelligence produced by these two organizations was code-named "Magic."

▲ William F. Friedman is often called the "father of American **cryptology**."

GOVERNMENT CODE AND CIPHER SCHOOL

As early as the 1920s, the British government concentrated all its code-breaking efforts in one place: the Government Code and Cipher School (GC&CS). Like the U.S. Cipher Bureau, the main task of GC&CS between the wars was deciphering diplomatic codes. However, as the threat of war increased, the code-breakers increasingly turned their attention to military ciphers. GC&CS's base was in London, but this was not a safe place for it to be if war broke out; the work of code-breaking needed to continue uninterrupted by possible enemy air attacks.

CAPTAIN RIDLEY'S SHOOTING PARTY

In 1938, the government acquired a house about 50 miles (80 kilometers) northwest of London. A large and rambling country estate, its name was Bletchley Park. A property developer had bought it for demolition and redevelopment, but then it mysteriously changed hands once again. In fact, although local people were unaware of it, MI6, the British secret intelligence service, had bought the house. This was to be the headquarters of GC&CS during the war. One reason for the choice of Bletchley Park as "Station X" (one of its code names) was its convenient geographical position. It was close to railroad lines going south to London, north to Birmingham, east to Cambridge, and west to Oxford, all in England.

▼ This photograph of Bletchley Park was taken in the 1960s.

Soon people began to arrive at Bletchley Park—a "shooting party," apparently hosted by a Captain Ridley. In fact, Captain Ridley was a naval officer with MI6 who organized the move of GC&CS out of London. As more people were brought in, it quickly became apparent that the house at Bletchley Park would not be big enough for all of the necessary personnel. Soon the grounds began to be filled with wooden huts to be used as self-contained "offices." Each hut had a number and, for security, the teams working in the huts were always known by their hut numbers—even if they later moved around.

HISTORY DETECTIVES: INTERNET RESEARCH

The Internet is a great resource for research, but it is also a place where anyone can post information. When you are researching a topic, you need to be careful to investigate the source of any relevant web sites, to make sure they are valid and reliable. Web site addresses give you useful clues about what kind of information they are likely to contain:

- Web sites ending in ".gov" are government sites, and they are often useful for statistics and reports.

- Sites ending in ".org" are often **nonprofit organizations**. You will need to assess these for the type of information they contain and any **bias** (prejudice toward a particular person or group).

- Sites ending in ".edu" are usually educational institutions.

You can also use trusted web sites such as the National Archives or the Library of Congress for access to vast amounts of useful information.

You can find out all about the history of Bletchley Park at: www.bletchleypark.org.uk.

WHAT KIND OF PEOPLE WERE THEY?

What kind of people were recruited to work as code-breakers in World War II? At Bletchley Park, many of the first people to arrive in 1939 had worked in Room 40 during World War I. They included Alastair Denniston, head of GC&CS, Dillwyn ("Dilly") Knox and Nigel de Grey (who had broken the Zimmermann telegram code), and Frank Birch. The code-breakers of Room 40 had mainly been language specialists, but Denniston decided that it was necessary to recruit people who specialized in other subjects. He looked to England's Oxford and Cambridge universities for brilliant mathematicians and scientists. During 1939, Peter Twinn, Gordon Welchman, and Alan Turing, all mathematicians, arrived at Bletchley Park. They were to play an essential role in the work of the years to come.

RECRUITING FOR BLETCHLEY

At first, there was a group of about 180 people working at Bletchley Park, but it quickly became clear that far greater numbers would be needed to deal with the challenge of Enigma. Denniston needed to recruit more **linguists** and mathematicians and, crucially, the huge numbers of support workers who were needed to keep the whole operation running smoothly. He needed secretaries, couriers (message-carriers), telephone operators, typists, and interpreters, as well as catering and security employees.

VERY SECRET...AND LOUSY PAY

One **veteran** of Bletchley Park recalls being offered a job there by Gordon Welchman. He remembered: "He couldn't tell me what it was, where it was, or anything of that kind, but he could say that it was very important, very interesting, and that the pay was lousy."

▲ This shows workers in Hut 3 at Bletchley Park. This was where intelligence information for the British army and air force was processed.

The search for people to work at Bletchley Park took both usual and unusual routes. Huge numbers of women were recruited to work there, many in clerical jobs. Many came from the women's armed services—the Women's Royal Naval Service (WRNS) and the Women's Auxiliary Air Force (WAAF). Some of them were civilians recruited from the Foreign Office. However, even these organizations could not fulfill the need for people with the right qualifications, so recruiters also looked for people who worked at banks and companies such as the John Lewis department stores. People already working at Bletchley Park often recommended friends or colleagues who they knew would be useful—and discreet. The numbers of employees rose steadily to reach about 7,000 at the beginning of 1944.

CHESS AND CROSSWORD PUZZLES

The recruiters at Bletchley Park became inventive at finding people who might be able to crack codes. People who were good at chess or at crossword puzzles were considered prime targets. Hugh Alexander worked for the John Lewis stores, but he also happened to be the British chess champion. He was recruited by Gordon Welchman, and he went on to work alongside Alan Turing in Hut 8 (see page 23). Welchman also recruited Stuart Milner-Barry, another chess champion and a friend of Hugh Alexander. In the following years, Milner-Barry and Welchman worked together closely in Hut 6.

▼ This building was Hut 3 at Bletchley Park.

Meanwhile, in January 1942, the *Daily Telegraph* newspaper announced a crossword puzzle competition. It offered a cash prize to anyone who could complete the *Telegraph* crossword in less than 12 minutes at a timed trial in the newspaper's offices. Those who managed it got more than the prize—they were also summoned to interviews for jobs at Bletchley Park.

HISTORY DETECTIVES:
THE "NEED TO KNOW"

Most people working at Bletchley Park knew little, if anything at all, of what was going on outside their own department. Everything was organized on a "need to know" basis. This is the memory of Professor I. J. (Jack) Good, a mathematician who worked with Alan Turing in Hut 8:

There is probably no one person who could give a reasonably comprehensive [full] account of any large project at Bletchley. People who were not at the top did not know much about matters that were not directly of their concern, and the people who were at the top were not fully aware of what was going on because of the complexity of the work.

BRITISH MATHEMATICIANS

The mathematicians who came to Bletchley Park were to play an essential part in cracking Enigma. The problem was that although they had the work of the Polish code-breakers to build on, this work had allowed the code-breakers to break only the early key systems used by the Germans. Once the Germans increased the levels of security for Enigma in 1939 (see page 12), new ideas were needed. Every time the key systems changed, or the Germans adapted the Enigma machines slightly, code-breakers had to break these new systems again. How Turing and his fellow mathematicians did this is the subject of pages 28–29.

WHO IN HISTORY

ALAN TURING
1912–1954
BORN: London, England

ROLE: In 1939, Turing went to work at Bletchley Park. He developed a powerful device, known as the Bombe, that helped crack the Enigma messages. His section in Hut 8 was responsible for decoding German naval and U-boat communications. After the war, Turing worked at Britain's National Physical Laboratory and then at Manchester University on a "universal machine"— a programmable computer. His huge contribution to code-breaking during the war was never publicly acknowledged in his lifetime, because he died before the secrecy surrounding Bletchley Park was brought to an end.

Did You Know?

Turing was a gifted runner and in 1948 might have been considered for the British Olympic marathon team if he had not had a leg injury.

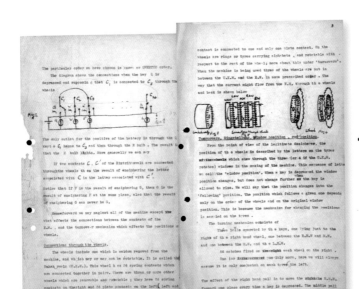

These are pages from the notes made by Turing on the Enigma machine between 1939 and 1942.

HISTORY DETECTIVES:
INSIDE HUT 8

We know something about the personalities in Hut 8 from an official report written by one of the team members, A. P. Mahon, in 1945. Called "The History of Hut Eight," the report was part of a batch of secret material that was not released for the public to read until 1996. In it, Mahon quotes a letter written on August 21, 1940, by Frank Birch:

> I'm worried about Naval Enigma. I've been worried for a long time, but haven't liked to say as much... Turing and Twinn are brilliant, but like many brilliant people, they are not practical. They are untidy, they lose things, they can't copy out right... Nor have they the determination of practical men.

Mahon's own explanation of this comment was that despite his brilliance, one of Turing's problems was his "almost total inability to make himself understood," and that he was a "lamentable explainer."

SIS AND OP-20-G

Meanwhile, in the United States, by the middle of 1939, there were fewer than 20 people working for William F. Friedman's Signal Intelligence Service (SIS) in Washington, D.C. When war broke out in 1939, the United States remained neutral. Nevertheless, the government decided to expand the SIS. By the time the United States entered the war in December 1941, the SIS employed about 500 people. In order to accommodate them all, in

WHO IN HISTORY

WILLIAM F. FRIEDMAN
1891–1969
BORN: Kishinev, Russia

ROLE: William F. Friedman had a background in science. He was studying genetics at Cornell University in Ithaca, New York, when he met Elizebeth Smith, a researcher into codes and ciphers at the privately run Riverbank Laboratories. Through her, Friedman became interested in cryptography. Elizebeth and William married in 1917 and worked together on all aspects of codes and code-breaking. Friedman became head of the SIS in 1929 and oversaw the move from pencil-and-paper code-breaking to using sophisticated machines, and mathematical processes, for both creating and cracking codes. He helped to develop SIGABA, the secure cipher machine used by the United States during World War II, in addition to training the team that broke the Japanese PURPLE code (see page 30).

Did You Know?

Elizebeth Friedman was just as much of a code-breaking pioneer as her husband. Among her many achievements, she broke the codes in letters sent by American businesswoman Velvalee Dickinson. Friedman's analysis revealed that Dickinson had been passing information to the Japanese about U.S. ship movements in Pearl Harbor. Based on this evidence, Dickinson was found guilty of spying.

July 1942, the U.S. Army moved the SIS to Arlington Hall Station (AHS)—formerly a girls' school. The demands of wartime code-breaking meant that by the middle of 1943, more than 2,000 people worked at AHS. The Navy, meanwhile, moved its code-breaking department (OP-20-G) to another girls' school—Mount Vernon Seminary, just outside Washington, D.C.

AMERICAN MATHEMATICIANS AND MAGICIANS

Mount Vernon Seminary became known as the Naval Communications Annex, although its Enigma office was nicknamed the Office of College Professors. The codes the mathematicians were working on were mainly Japanese diplomatic and naval messages. The intelligence produced from this code-breaking was known as "Magic"—possibly because in the 1930s, Friedman used to refer to his dedicated staff of code-breakers as "magicians"!

WOMEN AT WORK

During World War II, thousands of women worked in the U.S. code-breaking organizations. Many belonged to either the Army's Women's Army Auxiliary Corps (WAAC) or the Navy's Women Accepted for Voluntary Emergency Service (WAVES). Some of these women took the places of men who were on active service overseas. Women had to have mathematical and language skills to qualify, but above all they were required to be loyal and discreet. They were sworn to secrecy and warned that loose talk was considered treason—and punishable by death.

▼ Arlington Hall in Virginia was home to the U.S. Army's SIS from 1942.

"CARELESS TALK COSTS LIVES"

Winston Churchill, UK prime minister during the war, said of the workers at Bletchley Park that they were "the geese that laid the golden eggs—but never cackled." We have already seen that very few people at Bletchley Park knew much about the work that was going on beyond their own section. Even getting to Bletchley Park was shrouded in mystery. After arriving at Bletchley station, recruits were simply told: "You will find a telephone kiosk. Ring this number and await instructions." From the moment they were recruited, people were made aware of the highly sensitive nature of their work, and of its importance to the "war effort."

All workers at Bletchley Park had to sign the Official Secrets Act, the law that protects information related to national security in the United Kingdom. Employees were also instructed not to talk about their work at any time. The message that "careless talk costs lives" was so powerful that the security at Bletchley Park was never broken. The promise not to talk continued for many years after the war, until the secrets of Bletchley Park began to be told in the 1970s (see page 50).

HOW DO WE KNOW?

Following official orders, much of the material from Bletchley Park was destroyed at the end of the war to preserve secrecy (see page 48). However, there are a few accounts of the wartime activities of the code-breakers.

◀ This "Careless Talk" propaganda poster from the United Kingdom shows a soldier pulling a zipper across his mouth, to keep in any important military information.

"The History of Hut Eight" by A. P. Mahon, the head of Hut 8 from August 1944, is one example. Mahon wrote it in 1945 as a classified report—meaning it was secret and not available to the public. He starts by noting that the habits of secrecy mean that those working in Hut 8 "have never been enthusiastic keepers of diaries and log books and have habitually destroyed records when their period of utility [use] was over and it is the merest chance that has preserved a few documents of interest; hardly any of these are dated." As a result, he says that a "very large portion of this history is simply an effort of memory confirmed by referring to other members of the Section."

You can find the complete text of "The History of Hut Eight" at: www.ellsbury.com/hut8/hut8-001.htm.

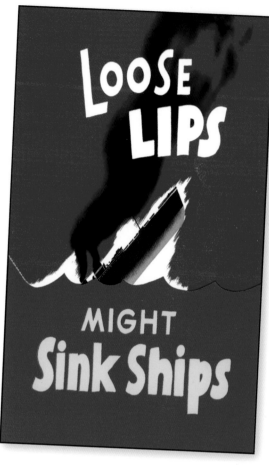

▲ "Loose Lips Might Sink Ships" was used on propaganda posters created by the U.S. Office of War Information.

HISTORY DETECTIVES:
INTERPRETING IMAGES

Primary source material includes all sorts of images, such as paintings, photos, posters, and movies. The propaganda posters shown here were produced during World War II. Their aim was to influence how people thought and behaved.

WHAT DID THEY DO TO BREAK THE CODES?

The German belief that the ciphers would remain invulnerable [unbreakable] was almost right, almost correct. The ciphers nearly escaped effective exploitation. In the case of the Enigma...the first solutions were made by hand by mathematicians relying on German operators' errors.

▲ This is an example of a Zygalski sheet, the perforated sheets used to crack Enigma ciphers.

This insight into the difficulty of breaking the Enigma code comes from a lecture given in 1993, by Harry Hinsley, who worked at Bletchley Park during World War II. The Germans firmly believed in the security of their military Enigma machines. Not only did the machines make use of the rotating "scramblers" described on page 8, but they also had a plugboard (called a "steckerbrett"), which allowed the operators to swap pairs of letters by inserting plugs into different holes. The combination of rotors and plug connections on the Enigma gave a total of 158 billion, billion different settings. The task of the code-breaker was to try to figure out which of these settings was being used.

THE POLISH CONTRIBUTION

In order to send and receive messages, the Germans distributed codebooks that typically showed a month's worth of settings for the scramblers and the plug connections, to be changed daily. The missing piece of information was the start position of the (usually three) rotors, which was changed for every message sent. The first breakthrough for the Polish code-breakers Marian Rejewski, Henryk Zygalski, and Jerzy Rozycki was when they realized that the Germans were sending this information twice, as the first six letters of any message. This was a major error on the Germans' part, and it eventually allowed Rejewski and his colleagues to decode the German communications.

BRAVE POLES

Not only did the Polish code-breakers give the British and French invaluable information about Enigma, but they also showed extreme bravery in protecting this information during the war. In 1943, the Germans captured Lieutenant-Colonel Langer and Major Maksymilian Ciezki, his colleague from the Cipher Bureau. Under severe interrogation, they did not give away the Polish and British successes in cracking Enigma—if they had, all the work of the code-breakers at Bletchley Park would have been for nothing.

By the time the Poles shared their work with the British and French in July 1939, they were able to hand over two replica Enigma machines, in addition to information detailing how they had broken the code up to that point. This included a system of **perforated** sheets developed by Zygalski, designed to decode the wheel settings, and a machine called the Bomba, designed by Rejewski. This machine provided the basis for the development of a device called a Bombe by Turing and Welchman (see page 33).

PURPLE

In the United States, the code-breakers were working on Japanese codes. The SIS had successfully decoded Japanese diplomatic messages during the 1930s, but in 1939, Japan introduced a new, more secure system. It was code-named "PURPLE" by the Americans. It took William F. Friedman and his team 18 months to crack this difficult code, in late 1940. They managed it by creating a replica of the Japanese machine.

Once PURPLE was broken, it allowed the SIS to read Japanese diplomatic communications throughout the war—although at times the code-breakers struggled to keep up with the workload. During 1940 and 1941, the SIS and OP-20-G cooperated by processing Japanese diplomatic messages on alternate days—the SIS on even dates, and OP-20-G on odd dates! But after the attack on Pearl Harbor, in Hawaii, the Navy code-breakers became too busy and gave up this arrangement.

▼ A Japanese bomber flies over Pearl Harbor during the attack in December 1941.

JN-25

The name given by code-breakers to the communications system used by the Imperial Japanese Navy during World War II was "JN-25." Work on this code started in 1940, but there was not enough progress to warn of the Japanese attack on the U.S. naval base at Pearl Harbor on December 7, 1941. It was this attack that brought the United States into World War II. The battle to crack JN-25 was undertaken not only in Washington, D.C., by OP-20-G, but also by the Navy unit ("Station Hypo") in Pearl Harbor, which was led by Commander Joseph Rochefort, a Japanese speaker and a gifted cryptologist.

As with Enigma, small security lapses gave the code-breakers the clues necessary to break JN-25. For example, messages often began with such phrases as "I have the honor to inform your Excellency." Knowing that the first letters of a message might be these words helped the code-breakers understand how that message had been coded. These small errors allowed the code-breakers to understand JN-25 sufficiently by 1942 to give warning of the attack on Midway Island (see page 42).

THE AMERICANS VISIT BLETCHLEY PARK

Even before the United States entered the war in 1941, the Americans and British had already agreed to cooperate and share code-breaking information. With the approval of the U.S. president, Franklin D. Roosevelt, a group of American code-breakers visited Bletchley Park in February 1941. They took with them a replica PURPLE machine, to help the British decipher Japanese communications. In return, they were given a tour of Bletchley Park and information about what was going on there. One of the Americans, Prescott Currier, later recalled: "We went everywhere, including Hut 6. We watched the entire operation and had all the techniques explained in great detail." In fact, the British were careful not to give away all their Enigma secrets because of concerns about U.S. security (see page 43).

Y-STATIONS

In the United Kingdom, it was Gordon Welchman who figured out a plan for the organization of Bletchley Park. The whole process started with the interception of German radio communications. This was done in listening stations all over the country, known as Y-stations. Employees worked eight-hour shifts, monitoring the airwaves day and night. It was tense and stressful work—it could be difficult to keep awake after many hours of hearing nothing but buzzing and **static**, but then suddenly have to concentrate to write down a message. The communications were sent in Morse code, which the interceptors wrote down on red, top-secret forms. This raw data was then sent to Station X as fast as possible, usually by motorcycle courier or **teleprinter**. Of course, the listeners had no idea that Station X was Bletchley Park, and they did not know if the information they were writing down was routine or extremely valuable.

▼ This diagram of Bletchley Park shows the location of the huts and intelligence units.

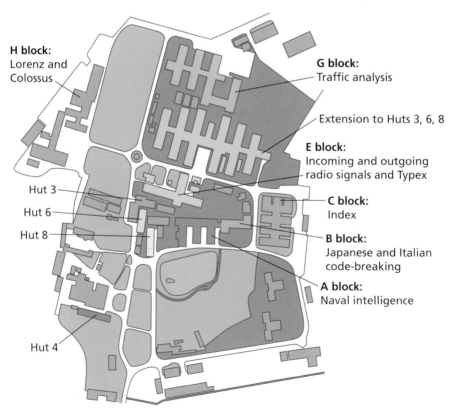

H block:
Lorenz and
Colossus

G block:
Traffic analysis

Extension to Huts 3, 6, 8

E block:
Incoming and outgoing
radio signals and Typex

Hut 3

Hut 6

Hut 8

C block:
Index

B block:
Japanese and Italian
code-breaking

A block:
Naval intelligence

Hut 4

HOW DID BLETCHLEY PARK WORK?

The Enigma teams worked in pairs—Hut 6 with Hut 3, and Hut 8 with Hut 4.

HUT 14: REGISTRY
Intercept data from Y-stations is logged in.

TRAFFIC ANALYSIS
Messages are carefully recorded and cross-referenced.

CODE-BREAKING HUTS: HUT 6 (ARMY AND AIR FORCE) AND HUT 8 (NAVY)

Intercept Room communicates with Y-stations about which radio networks to monitor, and what information to prioritize.

Machine Room is the nerve center of the code-breaking activity. This is where the teams figure out the settings ("keys") used by the Germans for each Enigma message.

Decoding Room deciphers messages using the keys found in the Machine Room.

INTELLIGENCE HUTS: HUT 3 (ARMY AND AIR FORCE) AND HUT 4 (NAVY)

The Watch translates messages from German into English.

The Advisers rewrite messages to conceal their sources and protect the work of the code-breakers. They also add any relevant notes or information from the index (see page 40).

The Index, for information storage, is constantly updated as new messages come in.

WHAT WAS THE BOMBE?

The Bombe was a machine devised by Turing and Welchman, based on an idea that came from the Polish code-breakers. Turing and Welchman were able to use **cribs**—common words or phrases that frequently came up in German communications—to guess parts of messages. They also exploited a weakness of the Enigma machine—that a letter could never be coded as itself. Using this information, they designed a machine that helped to speed up the Enigma code-breaking process by finding the daily key settings used by the Germans. The first successful Bombe was up and running in August 1940. More than 200 of these machines were made during the war.

NAVY CODES

Despite the success of the Bombe, British code-breakers were still finding German naval codes almost impossible to crack. The Germans used different Enigma settings sheets for different networks. The naval Enigma machines had more scramblers than those used by other networks, and the naval operators were carefully trained not to make errors.

U-BOAT THREAT

The need for naval intelligence was critical. The United Kingdom relied on supplies of food, oil, and other essential raw materials brought across the Atlantic Ocean. For safety, merchant ships sailed in groups, called **convoys**, protected by naval ships, but German U-boats were a constant threat. The U-boats attacked in groups known as packs, and in 1940 and 1941, they sank large numbers of Allied ships. The situation was becoming desperate—and it called for desperate measures.

OPERATION RUTHLESS

The code-breakers needed to know the German naval Enigma keys, but they were unable to crack them using methods that worked for other networks. So they decided to steal them. In September 1940, Lieutenant Commander Ian Fleming of British Naval Intelligence drew up a daring plan, code-named Operation Ruthless. He planned to crash a captured German plane in the English Channel, complete with a British, German-speaking crew. The crew would signal for help, then, when aboard the rescue ship, kill their German rescuers and seize the Enigma codebooks. The plan was never put into action because there were no suitable German ships in the English Channel. This episode only came to light when documents were released in 1996. We now know Ian Fleming as the author of the James Bond books!

The code-breakers did get their codebooks eventually—in the raid described on page 4. But breaking the naval codes continued to be a game of cat and mouse. Every time the Germans increased security, months of British work became useless, and the code-breakers had to start all over again.

▲ English novelist Ian Fleming is shown here in his study in 1958. He worked as a naval intelligence officer during World War II, an experience that provided him with the material for his books about James Bond.

HISTORY DETECTIVES: 56 YEARS LATER

This **excerpt** comes from one of the documents made available to the public in 1996. The document is a note written in 1940 by Frank Birch to the Admiralty (in charge of the British Royal Navy) after the cancellation of Operation Ruthless. A "pinch" refers to the stealing of the codebooks:

> *Turing and Twinn came to me like undertakers cheated of a nice corpse two days ago, all in a stew about the cancellation of Operation Ruthless. The burden of their song [their meaning] was the importance of a pinch [stealing the settings sheets]. Did the authorities realise that…there was very little hope, if any, of their deciphering current…enigma for months and months and months— if ever? Contrariwise, if they got a pinch—even enough to give a clue to one day's material, they could be pretty sure…of keeping going from day to day from then on.*

TUNNY AND FISH

For the most top-secret communications between army commanders and headquarters in Berlin, the Germans used Lorenz, an even more complicated cipher machine than Enigma. The messages produced by Lorenz were known at Bletchley Park as "Fish," and the machine was "Tunny." Two code-breakers, John Tiltman and Bill Tutte, made brilliant breakthroughs on the code during 1941 and 1942 using paper methods rather than machines. However, it was clear that a machine was needed to crack this code—a very large machine!

THE NEWMANRY

The task of creating a machine to defeat Tunny went to a University of Cambridge mathematician named Max Newman. His section became known as the Newmanry. Newman used some of Turing's ideas developed in the 1930s to design an electronic digital information machine— a computer. At first, no one believed that Newman's designs could be turned into a real machine. But Newman turned to a brilliant post office electrical engineer named Tommy Flowers.

▼ Workers from the Women's Royal Naval Service
  (WRNS) operate Colossus at Bletchley Park in 1944.

Flowers took Newman's plans and spent 10 months building the machine. The parts for the first "Colossus" arrived at Bletchley in December 1943. This machine was capable of huge amounts of mathematical work, allowing the code-breakers to crack the "Fish" code. By the end of the war, there were 10 Colossus machines at Bletchley Park.

HISTORY DETECTIVES:
REBUILDING THE COLOSSUS

At the end of the war, the Colossus machines and all the designs were destroyed (see page 48). Those who had worked on it were forbidden to talk about it. It was only in the 1970s that information about Colossus began to come out, and people realized that Bletchley Park had seen the first steps into the computer age.

In 1993, a computer engineer and historian named Tony Sale started a project to rebuild the Colossus machine. The only bits of information he had to go on were a few black-and-white photographs of Colossus taken during the war and some fragments of circuit diagrams.

Sale used the photos to create 3-D images on a computer. He also tracked down some of the engineers who had worked on Colossus to help him. He reconstructed the machine in H block at Bletchley Park—where the original Colossus was housed. Colossus was switched on in June 1996, and Tommy Flowers was there to see it!

You can read more about Lorenz, Colossus, and the rebuilding project at www.codesandciphers.org.uk/lorenz/index.htm.

WHO USED THE INFORMATION THEY FOUND?

We have seen how good the Allies were at breaking the codes of the **Axis Powers**, but what about the Axis code-breakers? How successful were they? In a lecture given in 1988, the British military historian Harry Hinsley pointed out that the two sides were fairly equally balanced at the beginning of the war. So, while breaking the Enigma code allowed the Allies to track the movements of the German air force in the Battle of Britain (see page 41), at the same time, German code-breakers were able to read large amounts of the Allied communications about naval traffic in the Atlantic Ocean.

▼ With its crew lined up on the deck and its officers in the tower, this German U-boat arrives at a naval base in 1939.

After the fall of 1941, however, the balance swung toward the Allies. While they continued to decipher the Enigma and Lorenz codes, Germany and Japan found it impossible to read the Allied ciphers (Typex and SIGABA). The fact that they could not crack the Allied codes may have convinced the Germans that, equally, the Allies were not able to read their communications. This may explain why they did not introduce more security measures to protect Enigma.

HOW IT WAS USED

Breaking the codes was only the first part of the story. *How* the intelligence was used was just as important. Distribution of Ultra intelligence from Bletchley Park was the job of the Special Liaison Units (SLUs). The task for the SLUs was to make sure Ultra intelligence went to the right people and that the source of the information was never given away. The commanders who received Ultra intelligence were not allowed to tell anyone where it had come from or act too obviously on it. The British often went to great lengths to disguise their use of Ultra. For example, if Ultra gave information about the location of U-boats in the Atlantic, the U-boats would not be attacked until a suitable cover story was in place. This could be a search plane that "luckily" flew over the area or a warship that "just happened" to spot the U-boats. Very few people knew how the information was obtained or its reliability.

BRITISH—AMERICAN RELATIONS

The British were not convinced that their American allies took security quite as seriously, which led to tension between the two sides. American visitors to Bletchley Park in 1942 complained about not being allowed to see some parts of the operation. But the need to win the battle against the German U-boats in the Atlantic led to cooperation between Bletchley Park and OP-20-G. In 1943, the British and the Americans signed an agreement to share responsibilities between Bletchley Park and Arlington Hall.

KEEPING TRACK OF ULTRA

Every day, huge amounts of information came in to Bletchley Park. In order to turn the deciphered messages into useful intelligence, it was often necessary to compare them or relate them to previously deciphered signals. This information was kept on cards, which were stored in indexes. There were several indexes, including:

- a general index concerned with the key contents of messages and facts of the Ultra intelligence
- a dictionary-type index of **jargon** and abbreviations, designed to help the code-breakers make sense of what they were reading
- an index that logged dates, times, locations, keys, and so on, of signals.

Think About This

The information storage revolution

The indexes at Bletchley Park were mostly created and stored by hand. By the end of the war, there were millions of cards in the indexes. How would all of this information be stored today?

The people who worked on the indexes were nearly all women, many with language degrees. The indexes helped to make useful intelligence from decoded signals, and it was often the indexers who spotted connections or trends in the information they were logging. Indexing continued around the clock at Bletchley Park. Read more at: www.bletchleypark.org.uk/edu/archives/gccscoll.rhtm.

THE "RED" KEY

When France fell to the Germans in June 1940, Britain prepared itself for a possible German invasion. But first, the Germans needed to take control of the skies over Britain, and this meant defeating the Royal Air Force. As the German air force, the Luftwaffe, prepared for the "battle for Britain," the Germans remained unaware that the code-breakers of Bletchley Park's Hut 6 had broken the "Red" key used by the Luftwaffe in May 1940. From that time onward, all of the Luftwaffe Enigma communications were monitored and read.

10, Downing Street,
Whitehall.

MOST SECRET.

September 27, 1940.

Dear C.

In confirmation of my telephone message, I have been personally directed by the Prime Minister to inform you that he wishes you to send him daily all the ENIGMA messages.

These are to be sent in a locked box with a clear notice stuck to it "THIS BOX IS ONLY TO BE OPENED BY THE PRIME MINISTER IN PERSON".

After seeing the messages he will return them to you.

Yours ever,

C.

P.S. As there will be no check possible here, would you please institute a check on receipt of returned documents to see that you have got them all back.

▲ British Prime Minister Winston Churchill (left) inspects maps with Admiral Bertram Ramsay in 1940. Churchill took great interest in Ultra intelligence and, in the letter to the right dated September 1940, he requested to see it.

ULTRA AND CHURCHILL

One person who took Ultra very seriously was Winston Churchill. In September 1940, he requested that all Enigma intelligence should be sent to him in a locked box with a note saying "THIS BOX IS ONLY TO BE OPENED BY THE PRIME MINISTER IN PERSON." At that time, the Battle of Britain was at its height. Churchill and the RAF relied on Ultra for estimates of the numbers of planes available to the Germans and the numbers shot down in the air battles over southern England. During the Blitz (German bombing) that followed the Battle of Britain in the fall of 1940, Ultra provided information about potential targets for bombing raids, although sometimes this information came too late to be of any use.

JAPANESE PLANS

In the United States, the code name "Ultra" was also used for some intelligence, in addition to "Magic." The breaking of JN-25 (see page 31) in 1942 allowed the American code-breakers, led by Commander Rochefort at Station Hypo, to decipher enough signals to know that the Japanese were planning a major naval attack.

Admiral Isoroku Yamamoto, who was in charge of the Imperial Japanese Fleet, knew that the attack on Pearl Harbor had crippled or destroyed many U.S. ships. Now he wanted to lure the rest of the U.S. fleet into a trap. He decided to attack Midway Island, at the far northwest of the Hawaiian chain. Yamamoto calculated that the Americans would send their fleet to defend Midway, giving him the opportunity to deliver a knockout blow.

▼ The U.S. aircraft carrier *Yorktown* receives a direct hit from a Japanese bomber in the Battle of Midway, June 1942. The black puffs here are exploding U.S. anti-aircraft shells.

ROCHEFORT'S PLAN

Rochefort and his team were able to tell Admiral Chester W. Nimitz, the U.S. Pacific fleet commander, the general outline of Yamamoto's plan and a rough timetable. However, they did not know where the Japanese intended to strike—the target was simply called "AF" in all Japanese communications. Rochefort guessed that it could be Midway—but Nimitz needed more than a guess. So, Rochefort came up with a plan. He sent an order to the commanding officer on Midway to broadcast a fake message that the island was running out of fresh water. Rochefort hoped the Japanese would pick up the message. The plan worked—a decoded Japanese signal clearly stated that "AF was running out of water." This proved that "AF" was in fact Midway.

THE *CHICAGO TRIBUNE* LEAK

The British military historian John Keegan later wrote of the Battle of Midway that it was "the most stunning and decisive blow in the history of naval warfare." Thanks to Magic intelligence, Nimitz was able to concentrate his limited forces and sink four Japanese aircraft carriers. However, a security leak nearly brought an end to Magic. On June 7, 1942, the *Chicago Tribune* published an article stating that the U.S. Navy had known about the Japanese plans in advance—effectively admitting that the Americans could read JN-25. Luckily, it seems that no Japanese— or German or Italian—spy read that paper, because the Japanese continued using JN-25 as before. The leak was traced to Commander Morton T. Seligman, an officer on a U.S. ship, who had shared a cabin with a reporter and talked too freely.

RISKING MAGIC

In 1943, Magic intelligence showed that Admiral Yamamoto was supposed to visit a Japanese naval base on the Solomon Islands on April 18. President Roosevelt ordered Nimitz to "Get Yamamoto." But there was a risk that attacking him would betray the fact that the United States was breaking JN-25 signals. But the plan went ahead, and Yamamoto was killed. The Japanese did not change JN-25.

FLOWERS'S DEADLINE

As soon as the first Colossus machine was up and running at Bletchley Park, Tommy Flowers came under huge pressure to produce more improved versions, as quickly as possible. Working night and day, Flowers and his team managed to get a Colossus mark (version) II working by the deadline of June 1, 1944. Although Flowers did not know it, the deadline was of huge significance. Only five days later, the Allied invasion of France began—the so-called **D-Day** landings in Normandy.

HISTORY DETECTIVES: THE TUNNY REPORT

In 1945, three Bletchley Park code-breakers—Jack Good, Donald Michie, and Geoffrey Timms—wrote the "General Report on Tunny." This excerpt describes Colossus in action:

> *It is regretted that it is not possible to give an adequate account of the fascination of a Colossus at work: its sheer bulk and apparent complexity; the fantastic speed of thin paper tape round the glittering pulleys...the wizardry of purely mechanical decoding letter by letter.*

▼ An American soldier is helped ashore on Omaha Beach in Normandy, France, during the D-Day landings in June 1944. This was one of the many operations during World War II where Ultra intelligence helped to save lives.

COLOSSUS AND D-DAY

Throughout 1944, the Allies prepared for the invasion of France with an elaborate campaign of deception. They used any means possible to convince the Germans that they were planning attacks on Norway, and on France in the Pas-de-Calais—the region of northern France that is closest to England. In fact, the actual attacks were to take place on Normandy, much further south. In June 1944, Ultra intelligence from Colossus confirmed that the deception had worked. It was clear that German leader Adolf Hitler was expecting an attack on the Pas-de-Calais.

After the D-Day landings, the Allies destroyed the telephone systems in northern France, forcing the Germans to use radio communications. Colossus allowed the code-breakers to keep up with this huge volume of traffic and, by the end of 1944, there were seven machines in action.

HISTORY DETECTIVES: SECONDARY SOURCES

A secondary source is a document (such as this book) that discusses and analyzes information originally presented elsewhere. It is a secondhand rather than a firsthand account. Virtually all the primary sources (plans, photographs, and so on) relating to Colossus were destroyed after the war. Perhaps as a result of this, and of the length of time that no one was allowed to discuss it, many myths have grown up about Colossus. Some secondary sources, including books, pamphlets, and web sites, have repeated this inaccurate information.

Some common Colossus myths:
- Alan Turing designed Colossus. (No, it was Tommy Flowers who designed and built it.)
- Colossus was used to decipher Enigma. (No, it was used to crack Tunny.)
- Colossus produced automatic translations of German into English. (No, it didn't!)

For information about all aspects of Colossus, go to: www.colossus-computer.com/colossus1.html.

WHAT HAPPENED TO THE CODE-BREAKERS AFTER THE WAR?

My sister used to come home with the tips of her fingers all blackened and I once asked her about it. She said "Never ask me what I'm doing and never ask me after the war because I can't tell you" and we never did.

This quotation comes from the sister of an employee at Bletchley Park. Everyone who worked at Bletchley Park had promised not to talk—and they kept that promise. As a result, many Bletchley Park employees had difficulty obtaining work after the war. They were unable to be open about the expertise they had acquired during the conflict. Nor could they expect to receive references or recommendations from superior officers, since the departments in which they worked did not officially exist. They had to accept when they agreed to work at Bletchley Park that they would not get any public recognition for their role in the war.

▼ In 2006, former Bombe operator Jean Valentine (her hand is seen here) visited the Bletchley Park Museum and her old machines.

There are tales of husbands and wives who worked in different departments in Bletchley Park and never spoke to each other of their time there, and of family members who died without ever talking about their experiences. Even when the story of Bletchley Park began to come out in the 1970s, some veterans found that they were unable to break the lifelong habits of secrecy.

> ## Think About This
>
> **Secrecy and social media**
> In our modern world of Twitter, Facebook, and other social media, do you think such secrecy would be possible today?

WHY KEEP THE SECRET?

Why was the work of Bletchley Park kept secret for so long? In the years after the war, the ability to decipher Enigma and Tunny remained very useful. These codes were still used by countries all over the world. Only the British and Americans knew that these codes were crackable, and they kept this knowledge to themselves. Another reason for continued secrecy was the Cold War—the period of distrust and tension between the United States and its allies and the **Soviet Union**. The Cold War started after the end of World War II and continued until the Soviet Union collapsed in 1991.

WHAT HAPPENED TO BLETCHLEY PARK?

After the war, the code-breakers moved out of Bletchley Park, first to Middlesex, England, and then to new headquarters in Cheltenham, England. The UK Post Office, and later British Telecom, used Bletchley Park as a training center. By the 1990s, the house had fallen into disrepair, and the UK government decided to sell it. In 1991, it was at risk of demolition. However, many people felt that Bletchley Park should be saved as a tribute to those who had worked there, and as a place to educate people about what had happened there. After a lot of hard work, this is what happened. You can find out more about Bletchley Park today at: www.bletchleypark.org.uk.

GETTING RID OF THE EVIDENCE

When the war ended in 1945, Churchill ordered the destruction of much of the equipment and information at Bletchley Park. All of the 200 Bombes were eventually destroyed. Similarly, all but two of the Colossus machines were broken up and taken to the new Government Communications Headquarters (GCHQ)—the new name for GC&CS—in Middlesex, England. It seems they were used for a time after the war before, being dismantled in the 1950s and 1960s.

Tommy Flowers was ordered to destroy all the designs and plans for Colossus. He later wrote: "'That was a terrible mistake. I was instructed to destroy all the records, which I did. I took all the drawings and the plans and all the information about Colossus on paper and put it in the boiler fire. And saw it burn."

RECONSTRUCTION OF THE BOMBE

In the 1990s, a computer engineer named John Harper led a project to rebuild a Bombe. The team of volunteers who worked on the project had a complicated task piecing together the available information about the Bombe. There were a few photos of Bombes, as well as around 4,000 drawings of Bombe parts that had been sent to GCHQ after the war. Trying to piece all these drawings together was, according to Harper, like "being given four jigsaw puzzles all mixed up together and from which one picture has to be constructed." They also relied on the expertise of those who actually worked on Bombes during the war—the engineers who helped to build them and the WRNS who operated them.

The rebuilt Bombe was officially switched on at Bletchley Park in 2007. For the first time in 60 years, Bletchley Park re-created the way the "unbreakable" Enigma code was broken using functioning World War II equipment. The public can now hear the sound of the Bombe. It was, and is again, a noisy machine.

As part of the museum's exhibit, the British Computer Society also recorded the memories of some of the women who operated the Bombe. These **oral histories** can provide an important insight into what life was like at Bletchley Park during the war.

WHO IN HISTORY

THOMAS FLOWERS
1905–1998
BORN: London, England

ROLE: Flowers designed and built Colossus, the world's first programmable computer. Before the war, Flowers worked at the UK Post Office research station at Dollis Hill in London, developing electronics systems. In 1943, he began work on a machine to decipher the Lorenz system used by the German high command. Colossus was installed at Bletchley Park in 1944. After the war, Flowers was unable to reveal any of his work on Colossus. He went back to the Post Office and pioneered the use of electronic phone exchanges. Only after the 1970s, when information about Colossus began to come out, was his huge contribution to computing acknowledged.

Did You Know?

Flowers used his own money to help finance the building of Colossus. He received very little pay for his war work—barely enough to cover his expenses. If he could have used the knowledge he had developed during the war, he would probably have been a very rich man—but this was out of the question at the time.

THE SECRET IS OUT

British secrecy about Ultra was finally lifted in 1974. In that year, Frederick W. Winterbotham published the first account of Ultra in his book *The Ultra Secret*. Winterbotham had been the head of the Special Liaison Units (SLUs) at Bletchley Park during the war. In fact, he was not the first to go public about Enigma. A year earlier, a French intelligence officer named Gustave Bertrand had published *Enigma or the Greatest Enigma of the War of 1939–1945*, which told the story of Enigma from the time of the Polish code-breakers. But since the book was published in French, it did not have an immediate impact in the United Kingdom.

THE ULTRA SECRET

Winterbotham knew that other historians and writers were also interested in the secret wartime history of Bletchley Park, and that other accounts would be published eventually. He wrote mainly from memory, since all documents relating to the activities at Bletchley Park were still classified (top secret) at that time. His book provoked some very strong reactions. Some Bletchley Park veterans disapproved of his breaking the secrecy around Ultra, even so long after the event. Also, Winterbotham was not himself a code-breaker, and many people found fault with his account of the code-breaking processes at Bletchley Park. Others pointed to factual inaccuracies in his writing. For example, he wrote that decoded Enigma signals had provided clear warning of the bombing of Coventry, England, during the Blitz of 1940, but that Churchill chose not to act on this warning because of the danger of revealing that the British were cracking Enigma. Many historians have since shown that this was not the case.

ENIGMA

Since the publication of *The Ultra Secret,* there have been many more books telling the story of the World War II code-breakers, from many different points of view. In 2001, a movie was released called *Enigma*. British playwright Tom Stoppard adapted a novel by Richard Harris. It is set during a time when code-breakers at Bletchley Park are struggling to read the U-boat Enigma signals. Although the movie is fiction, it shows the work of the code-breakers in some detail.

▲ This still from the movie *Enigma* is set in March 1943, just as the Germans changed their U-boat codes. This image shows the Bombe machines that were re-created for the movie.

HISTORY DETECTIVES: ORAL HISTORY

I help the old to remember, and the young to understand.

"Our Secret War" is a British oral history project that records and films interviews with World War II veterans. Now that secrecy is no longer an issue, many veterans feel able to talk freely, some for the first time, about their experiences. These interviews will provide important archive material for future generations. "Our Secret War" has interviewed many men and women who worked at Bletchley Park and in the Y-stations. You can find out more at: www.our-secret-war.org.

AFTER THE WAR

In the United States at the end of the war, there were many thousands of people working at Arlington Hall and for OP-20-G (estimates are around 10,000 in each organization). When the fighting stopped, there was no longer any need for such intense code-breaking, and many workers lost their jobs in the general **demobilization** that followed. The Americans at Bletchley Park also returned home, many with extremely fond memories of their time working there. One of these code-breakers, Bill Bundy, later said of his time there: "Nothing gave the total personal satisfaction that Hut 6 did. Because this was a totally dedicated group working together in absolutely remarkable teamwork."

THE NSA

There were many issues to be considered after the war ended. Would the cooperation and intelligence-sharing agreed between the Americans and the British continue after the war? Would the U.S. Army and Navy intelligence agencies need to work more closely together? What new machines would need to be developed for code-breaking? In fact, the United States and the United Kingdom did agree to continue their joint relationship after the

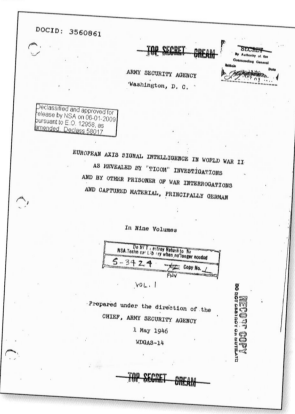

▲ This shows a declassified NSA document.

war, not spying on the Germans or Japanese this time, but rather on their former ally, the powerful Soviet Union. In the United States, budget cuts and the need to coordinate intelligence at a national level eventually led to the founding of the National Security Agency (NSA) in 1952.

HISTORY DETECTIVES:
DECLASSIFIED NSA DOCUMENTS

Some interesting information about Bletchley Park has come from documents that have been declassified (officially declared no longer secret) by the NSA. In 1995, a review of the U.S. Freedom of Information Act led to the release of documents about Colossus and Fish, written by the Americans who were stationed at Bletchley Park during the war. Some of these documents helped Tony Sale to piece together his reconstructed Colossus machine (see page 37). You can search and read many original documents on the NSA site, including:

- the original agreements signed by the United Kingdom and the United States in 1943 (see page 39) were declassified in 2010: www.nsa.gov/public_info/declass/ukusa.shtml

- examples of signal intelligence from World War II that were declassified in 2009: www.nsa.gov/public_info/declass/european_axis_sigint.shtml.

NAVAJO CODE–TALKERS

The Navajo code-talkers returned home after the war and kept silent. Their code had proved so valuable during the war that it remained top secret. It was not until 1968 that the code was declassified, and the Navajo were finally allowed to talk about the role they had played in World War II.

You can find out more about the Navajo code-talkers at: www.navajocodetalkers.org.

WHY WAS THEIR WORK SIGNIFICANT?

The official history of British intelligence in World War II was written by Harry Hinsley in several volumes, the first being published in 1979. In Hinsley's opinion, the use of Ultra intelligence shortened the length of the war by "not less than two years and probably by four years." Similarly, Magic played a huge part in the war in the Pacific Ocean.

ULTRA AND THE U-BOATS

There were many areas of the war in which Ultra intelligence was very important, such as the campaigns in North Africa and the Mediterranean. However, one of the most dramatic roles it played was in the Battle of the Atlantic between Allied shipping and the U-boats. Winston Churchill wrote after the war, "The only thing that ever really frightened me during the war was the U-boat peril."

The United Kingdom would not have survived the war without the food, raw materials, equipment, and troops that made the perilous journey across the Atlantic Ocean. Despite traveling in convoys, the Allied ships were extremely vulnerable to U-boat attack. The tactic used by the German naval command was for U-boats to hunt singly for Allied convoys. Once a convoy was located, the U-boat continued to shadow it while signaling for reinforcements. When all the U-boats were collected together in what the Germans called a "wolf pack," they would attack.

This technique was highly successful. However, it did rely on extremely good communications, and the U-boats used Enigma to code their messages. The German naval Enigma codes were very difficult to crack, and during the first half of 1941, the situation became serious for the Allies after the loss of huge numbers of ships. But once Ultra intelligence was available, from July 1941, the drop in the number of ships sunk was immediate—it was possible to reroute the convoys away from the U-boats. Unfortunately, the flow of Ultra intelligence stopped once again in 1942 (see the box on page 55).

▲ This Allied convoy sets sail in 1942. It was important to maintain the flow of supplies across the Atlantic Ocean between the United States and United Kingdom.

GERMAN SUSPICIONS

In February 1942, the German commander of the U-boats, Admiral Karl Dönitz, became suspicious that the British were reading U-boat Enigma signals. Although he never found out the truth, he nevertheless increased security. Suddenly, overnight, the code-breakers at Bletchley Park were unable to decipher any U-boat communications. It took until the end of 1942 for the British code-breakers to crack the new U-boat codes.

The use of Ultra to contain the U-boat threat in the Battle of the Atlantic meant that the Allies were able to go ahead with their plans for the D-Day landings in 1944. Again, experts think that this would have been impossible without the use of intelligence. This is the opinion of a German military historian, Jürgen Rohwer:

> I am sure that without the work of many unknown experts at Bletchley Park...the turning point of the Battle of the Atlantic could not have come as it did in May 1943, but months, perhaps many months, later. In that case the Allied invasion of Normandy could not have been possible in June 1944.

THE BIRTH OF THE COMPUTER

In 1943, the U.S. Army asked a team at the University of Pennsylvania to design a machine to help them calculate the information needed for firing artillery (big guns). This machine was the Electronic Numerical Integrator and Computer (ENIAC). The existence of ENIAC was revealed to the public in 1946, and this "giant brain" caught people's imaginations. It was described as the world's first electronic digital computer.

How did Tommy Flowers feel about ENIAC? Professor Jack Copeland is director of the Turing Archive for the History of Computing and a leading Turing expert. He interviewed Flowers many times, and he records Flowers's feelings in his book *Colossus: The Secrets of Bletchley Park's Codebreaking Computers*:

> When after the war ended I was told that the secret of Colossus was to be kept indefinitely I was naturally disappointed. I was in no doubt, once it was a proven success, that Colossus was an historic breakthrough, and that publication would have made my name in scientific and engineering circles—a conviction confirmed by the reception accorded to ENIAC, the U.S. equivalent made public just after the war ended. I had to endure all the acclaim given to that enterprise without being able to disclose that I had anticipated it. What I lost in personal prestige…can now only be imagined… I accepted the situation philosophically and…lost any concern about what might happen in the future.

It was only as information about Colossus began to come out in the 1970s that history could be rewritten. But according to Professor Copeland, Churchill's decision to destroy Colossus after the war was a major setback for the history of computing.

TURING AND ACE

For Turing, Colossus showed the speed and reliability of electronics. The idea he had been thinking about since the 1930s was for a "universal machine"—one that made use of coded instructions stored in its memory to carry out many different tasks. After the war, Turing was invited to work at the National Physical Laboratory in England in order to develop an electronic stored-program digital computer. Known as the Automatic Computing Engine, or ACE, it was the fastest computer of its time.

▲ This was the first demonstration of the pilot ACE at the National Physical Laboratory in December 1950.

BLETCHLEY PARK LEGACY

For many who worked at Bletchley Park, their time there was an extremely significant part of their lives. The wide range of people, interests, and talents made for a fascinating mix. For veterans such as Mavis Batey, it opened her eyes to the possibilities beyond the war. She said, "I was quite happy to have a bash [to try]... And that was what I realized was a gift, a legacy of Bletchley. You either do it or you don't, but no one else is going to do it if you don't."

TIMELINE

1917	Room 40 deciphers the Zimmermann telegram
1918	Arthur Scherbius invents the Enigma machine
1919	The U.S. Cipher Bureau is set up in New York City
1926	German armed forces begin to use a military version of Enigma
1929	The U.S. Cipher Bureau closes down; William F. Friedman becomes head of the SIS
1930s	Polish cryptographers work on breaking the Enigma code
1931	Herbert Yardley publishes *The American Black Chamber*
1938	The British government buys Bletchley Park
1939	*July:* Poles meet with the British and French to share their Enigma secrets *Sept. 1:* Germany invades Poland; Great Britain and France declare war on Germany
1940	*May:* Bletchley Park breaks the "Red" key used by the Luftwaffe; Bombe becomes operational at Bletchley Park *Aug.:* Battle of Britain begins, followed by the Blitz into 1941 *Late 1940:* American code-breakers break the Japanese PURPLE code
1941	*Feb.:* American code-breakers visit Bletchley Park *May:* The Royal Navy seizes German naval Enigma codebooks *Dec. 7:* Japan attacks the U.S. naval base at Pearl Harbor, Hawaii; the United States enters the war

1942	**June:** Battle of Midway
	June 7: *Chicago Tribune* article is published
	July: The SIS moves to Arlington Hall Station

1943	The Battle of Atlantic ends with heavy U-boat losses
	April 18: Japanese Admiral Yamamoto is killed after the United States deciphers signals about his movements
	Dec.: The first Colossus machine arrives at Bletchley Park

| 1944 | **June 1:** Successful installation of Colossus mark II |
| | **June 6:** Allies invade Normandy (D-Day landings) |

| 1945 | **May:** End of the war in Europe |
| | **Aug.:** War ends in the Pacific after atomic bombs are dropped on Hiroshima and Nagasaki, Japan |

| 1946 | **Feb.:** ENIAC is revealed to the public |
| | **April:** GC&CS leaves Bletchley Park and becomes GCHQ |

| 1950 | Turing's Automatic Computing Engine (ACE) runs its first program |

| 1974 | Publication of *The Ultra Secret* by Frederick W. Winterbotham |

| 1991 | Bletchley Park is saved from demolition |

| 1996 | Tony Sale's replica Colossus is switched on at Bletchley Park |

| 2007 | The rebuilt Bombe is switched on at Bletchley Park |

GLOSSARY

Allies at the start of World War II, the main Allies were France, Poland, and the United Kingdom and its empire, including Canada, Australia, and India. The United States and the Soviet Union joined the Allies in 1941.

ambassador government representative who is stationed in a foreign country

Axis Powers in World War II, the main Axis Powers were Germany, Italy, and Japan

bias having an unfair or unbalanced opinion

bureau office or department

cipher system that replaces one letter with another

cipher machine machine that turns plain text into cipher

code use of symbols or groups of letters to represent words or phrases

convoy group of vehicles, often ships, that travel together for protection

crib in cryptography, a crib is a common word or phrase that frequently comes up and provides a way into a code

cryptographer someone who specializes in writing or deciphering code

cryptography science of writing or deciphering code

cryptology another word for the science of writing or deciphering code

D-Day military term for the day an operation starts. The best-known use of the term is for the Normandy landings in June 1944, when the Allies attacked German-occupied France.

decipher convert from code to plain text

demobilization process of disbanding troops back to civilian life after the end of a conflict

encrypt turn something into code

excerpt short extract from a book, a song, or a movie

Great Depression economic crisis that began in 1929 in the United States and continued throughout the 1930s

intelligence material or information that has political or military value

intercept listen secretly to a signal or message

jargon specialized language used by a particular trade or group

linguist someone who specializes in speaking and understanding different languages

nonprofit organization organization such as a charity or a school in which any money made goes back into the organization

oral history collection and study of historical information by interviewing and recording people using audiotapes and videotapes or by writing down their words

perforate make holes in something

reconnaissance getting information by visual observation

replica copy

sabotage deliberately destroy or disrupt something

Soviet Union Union of Soviet Socialist Republics (USSR), the communist state that existed between 1922 and 1991. Modern-day Russia was part of the USSR.

static on a radio, a type of electronic noise or interference

telegram message sent by telegraph

teleprinter system of sending and receiving messages by typewriter, through the telephone system, or by other means

U-boat (stands for the German *Unterseeboot*) German submarine

veteran person who has had long experience in a particular field, especially in the armed forces

wireless process of using radio waves to transmit signals

FIND OUT MORE

BOOKS

Gregory, Jillian. *Breaking Secret Codes* (Making and Breaking Codes). Mankato, Minn.: Edge, 2010.

Langley, Andrew. *Codes and Codebreaking* (Spies and Spying). Mankato, Minn.: A+/Smart Apple Media, 2010.

Santella, Andrew. *Navajo Code Talkers* (We the People). Minneapolis: Compass Point, 2004.

Scott, Cory. *Spies and Code Breakers: A Primary Source History* (In Their Own Words). Pleasantville, NY: Gareth Stevens, 2009.

WEB SITES

www.archives.gov/publications/prologue/2001/winter/navajo-code-talkers.html

Learn more about the Navajo code-talkers at this National Archives site.

www.colossus-computer.com/colossus1.html

The story of Bletchley Park's code-breaking computers can be found here.

www.counton.org/explorer/codebreaking/index.php

Codes and code-breaking are explained on this web site.

www.cryptomuseum.com/index.htm

The Crypto Museum is an online museum all about cipher machines.

www.nsa.gov/about/cryptologic_heritage/

Learn more about the history and importance of cryptology in the United States at this National Security Agency (NSA) site.

www.turingarchive.org

The Turing Digital Archive has many letters, photographs, and memoirs of Alan Turing.

PLACE TO VISIT
National Cryptologic Museum
8290 Colony Seven Road
Annapolis Junction, Maryland 20701
www.nsa.gov/about/cryptologic_heritage/museum/index.shtml

OTHER TOPICS TO RESEARCH
There are many interesting topics related to the wartime codes. Start
with the suggestions below and discover which area holds the most
interest for you.

Who invented the computer?
As we have seen, it is a story that is complicated by the secrecy
surrounding the code-breakers of World War II. Find out more about
Turing, ENIAC, and ACE. A good place to start is www.turing.org.uk/turing/
scrapbook/computer.html.

Ultra information:
Ultra information was used in many areas of the war not covered in this
book. You could find out about its use at the Battle of Cape Matapan in
1941 and in North Africa in 1942.

Codes throughout history:
Codes and ciphers have been used throughout history and across cultures.
Can you find out more about the ways in which codes have developed over
the centuries? You could focus your research on how they have been used
in times of war.

INDEX